Native Crafts

Inspired by
North America's First Peoples

Written by Maxine Trottier
Illustrated by Esperança Melo

KIDS CAN PRESS

To the memory of my ancestor
Margeurite Ouabankikove

I wish to thank Ronald Doyle, Ann Fantz, Mary Elijah,
Cynthia Smith and Pat Cornelius for their assistance
and wisdom in this project

Text © 2000 by Maxine Trottier
Illustrations © 2000 by Esperança Melo

Kids Can Press acknowledges the support of the Government of Canada,
through the BPIDP, for our publishing activity. Canadä

Published in Canada by
Kids Can Press Ltd.
29 Birch Avenue
Toronto, ON M4V 1E2

Published in the U.S. by
Kids Can Press Ltd.
4500 Witmer Industrial Estates
Niagara Falls, NY 14305-1386

Edited by Laurie Wark
Designed by Karen Powers
Printed in Hong Kong by Wing King Tong Company Limited

CM 00 0 9 8 7 6 5 4 3 2 1
CM PA 00 0 9 8 7 6 5 4 3 2 1

Canadian Cataloguing in Publication Data

Trottier, Maxine
    Native crafts : inspired by North America's First Peoples

(Kids can do it)
1-55074-854-8 (bound)   1-55074-549-2 (pbk.)

1. Handicraft – Juvenile literature. 2. Indians of North America – Art – Juvenile
literature. 3. Indians of North America – Costume and adornment – Juvenile literature.
I. Melo, Esperanca. II. Title. III. Series.

TT160.T76 2000   j745.5   C99-932117-X

Kids Can Press is a Nelvana company

Contents

Introduction

If you could step back in time and walk across what we now call North America, you would find a very different place from what you see today. No highways cut across the land. There were no cities or stores. Yet the First Peoples who lived here had all they needed to make their clothing and homes, to feed their bodies as well as their spirits.

Aboriginal peoples learned to use the things they found in nature. Dolls and moccasins were different all across the land depending on what materials were available. Some of the items crafted were necessary for daily life. Other objects were used in ceremonies or as ornaments. Whether it was a bowl or a basket, a drum or a necklace, each thing was precious for the purpose it served as well as the time it took to create.

Today many people still create these traditional crafts. Nothing can

substitute for being taught by a traditional artist, but in these pages you will see how to adapt the methods Aboriginal people historically used to make your own useful and lasting objects. There are new techniques and materials, but what lies at the heart of the making of Aboriginal art and crafts has never changed. It is the handing down of ideas from one person to another. In this book, a small part of this tradition is passed on to you.

Traditional territories

In some cases, ancestral lands changed through history. This map shows the traditional territories of the peoples named in this book. Each community had its own way of life. But, because some lived in the same climate and regions, the peoples in these areas had things in common. They had similar foods, homes, styles of clothing and crafts.

- The Southeast
- The Southwest
- The Plains
- Plateau and Basin
- California
- The Northwest Coast
- The Subarctic
- The Arctic
- The Northeast

1. Aleut
2. Apache
3. Cayuse
4. Cherokee
5. Cheyenne
6. Chippewa
7. Crow
8. Dakota
9. Fox
10. Haida
11. Hidatsa
12. Hopi
13. Inuit
14. Inupiat
15. Iroquois (St. Lawrence)
16. Kiowa
17. Kutchin
18. Kwakiutl
19. Makah
20. Mi'kmaq
21. Mohave
22. Nez Perce
23. Oneida
24. Penobscot
25. Pima
26. Pueblo
27. Sauk
28. Seneca
29. Tlingit
30. Tsimshian
31. Yuma
32. Zuni
33. Wintu

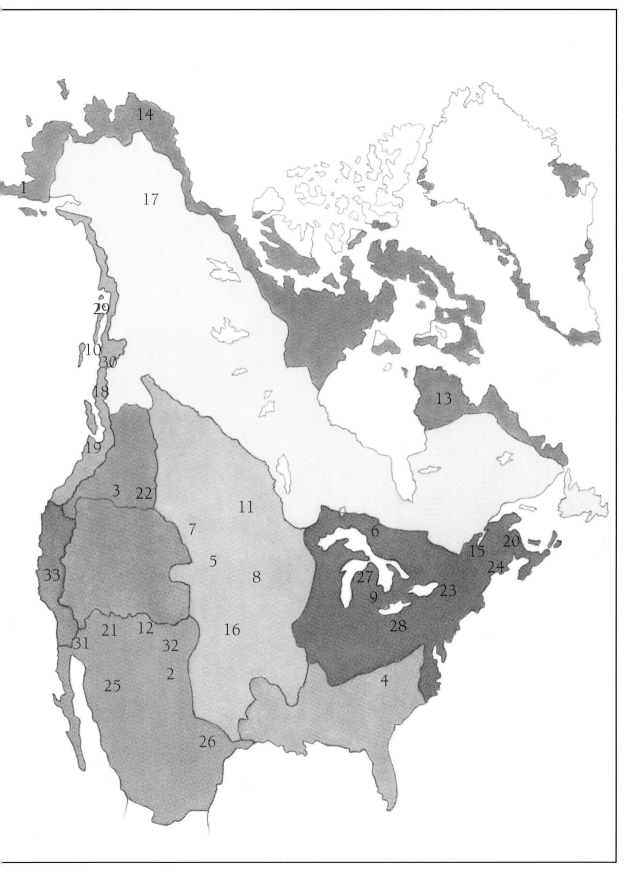

Seed and bead jewelry

Many Aboriginal peoples have historically grown crops. Corn, beans and squash are still referred to as the Three Sisters by the Iroquois. Seeds from vegetables were saved each year for planting in the spring, but there were other uses for them as well. Many peoples used seeds to make jewelry.

YOU WILL NEED

- seeds from sunflowers or from fruits and vegetables such as squash, melon or pumpkin
- scissors and a ruler
- a needle and beading thread
- beads such as E beads
- white glue or clear nail polish

1 Ask an adult to help you cut the fruit or vegetables in half and scoop out the seeds. Clean the seeds and spread them out on plates or baking sheets. Let them air-dry for a few days or have an adult place them in the oven on low for several hours.

2 Cut a length of doubled thread for a necklace or bracelet. You will need about 60 cm (24 in.) for a necklace or 25 cm (10 in.) for a bracelet. Thread the needle and tie a double knot at one end of the thread.

3 Decide on a pattern that alternates the seeds and beads.

4 Thread seeds onto the needle one at a time. Pull them down to the end of the thread. Then thread on beads and pull them down so that they touch the seeds.

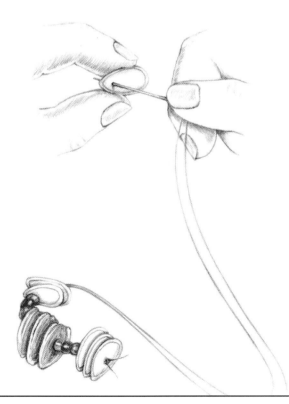

5 Continue threading on seeds and beads. Double knot the ends of the necklace or bracelet together. Secure the knot with a dab of glue or nail polish.

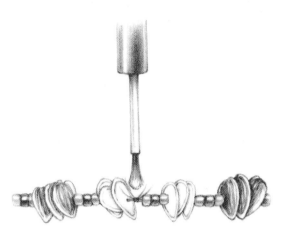

OTHER IDEAS

• Paint the seeds different colors before threading them.

• Try different-sized beads, such as seed beads or pony beads.

Bear claw necklace

Shells, animal claws, carved bone and stone were all used for making jewelry. The Cheyenne and Fox made necklaces and leg belts of animal claws, beads and small metal cones. This jewelry was often worn for ceremonies or special meetings. It could show to which clan you belonged or your position among your people. The designs might represent an event that had occurred in your life.

YOU WILL NEED

- self-hardening clay (available at craft supply stores)
- toothpicks
- acrylic paint and a small paintbrush
- strong cord, leather lace or ribbon
- a darning needle
- large beads, such as pony beads (optional)

1 To make bear claws, roll pieces of clay into teardrop shapes. Bend them into curves.

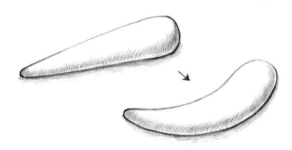

2 Poke a wet toothpick through the top of each claw, turning the toothpick as you push it in and out. Lay the claws on a plate to dry.

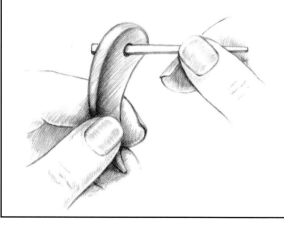

3 For round beads, roll clay into small balls. Poke a wet toothpick through to make a hole in each bead. Let the beads dry.

4 To make square beads, roll balls of clay. Use four fingers to press the balls into cubes. Make a hole in each bead and let them dry. Try making cylindrical or triangular beads as well.

5 To make a pendant, roll a 2.5-cm (1-in.) ball of clay. Flatten it into a disk and smooth it on all sides with wet fingers.

6 Roll out a small sausage of clay and smooth it onto the top of the pendant for a hanger. Make sure no seams show. Let the pendant dry.

7 Paint the claws, beads and pendant and let the paint dry. You can create your own designs or use something you have seen in nature.

8 Decide on a pattern, and use the darning needle to string beads onto a piece of cord that is long enough to slip over your head. Include pony beads, if you like. Tightly double knot the ends of the cord.

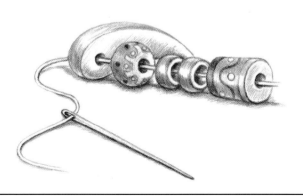

Rosette necklace

The designs that were traditionally used on clothing and household objects were often works of art. Leggings, shirts, moccasins and pouches might be painted or beaded. The Crow and Kiowa painted their tepees. The Cayuse even beaded collars for their horses. The Chippewa and other peoples made bead rosettes.

1 Draw two circles with a diameter of 5 cm (2 in.) each onto the felt. Cut out both circles and set one aside.

2 Decide on a pattern of colors for the rings of beads that will make up the rosette.

3 Thread the needle and knot the thread. Sew one bead onto the center of the felt. Poke the needle back up close to the bead.

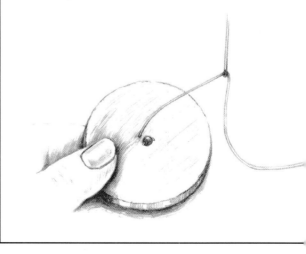

4 Thread on eight beads to make a circle around the first bead. Close the circle of beads by running the needle through the first two beads.

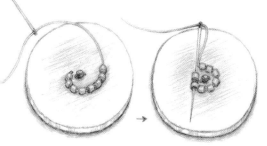

5 Place the circle of beads on the felt around the center bead. Attach the circle by sewing a stitch every two or three beads over the thread on which the beads have been threaded.

6 Continue adding rings of beads until you reach the edge of the felt circle.

7 Place the second felt circle over the back of the rosette. Use small stitches along the edges of both circles to sew them together.

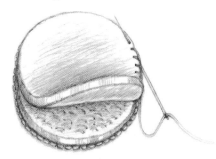

8 Measure a piece of thread to make a necklace long enough to slip over your head. String beads onto the thread. Close the necklace by running the thread back through the first two beads and sew the necklace onto the rosette.

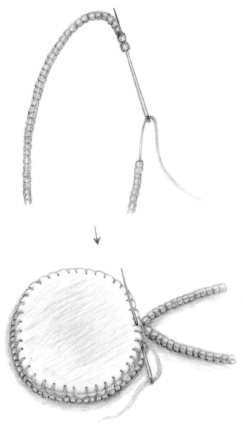

Beaded bracelet

Beadwork is one of the oldest forms of Aboriginal art. Beads of shell, bone and antler were strung on sinew or hide laces. Some beadwork was done on looms, but other bead-weaving was done by hand. The Mi'kmaq, Sauk and Fox used beads to weave bracelets and armbands.

1 Cut six 60-cm (24-in.) lengths of thread. Four will be one color and two will be the second color. Pair off the strands by color and thread a pair through each needle.

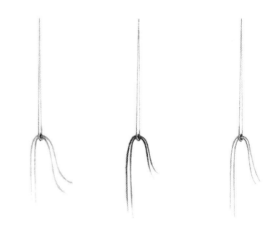

2 Thread four beads onto each needle. Tie all the threads together at one end, leaving a 5-cm (2-in.) tail.

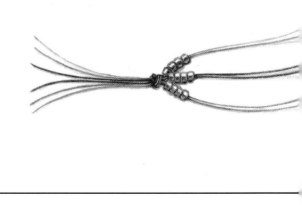

3 Set the bracelet on a flat surface. Thread the top needle between the threads of the middle and bottom strands. The top strand is now the bottom strand.

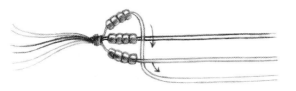

4 Thread four more beads onto each needle. You may alternate colors to make a pattern.

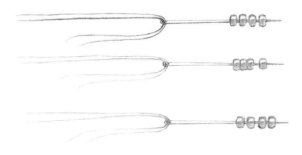

5 Thread the top needle between the threads of the middle and bottom strands. The top strand is again now the bottom strand.

6 Repeat steps 4 and 5 until you have enough sections to go around your wrist.

7 Remove the needles and tie the threads as close as possible to the last section of beading. Trim the thread, leaving a 5-cm (2-in.) tail.

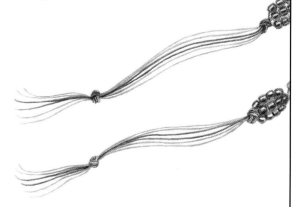

8 Use the two tails of thread to tie the bracelet around your wrist.

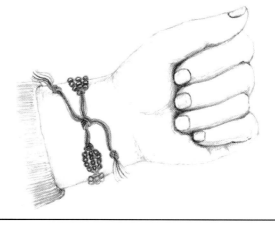

Clay pinch pot

Pottery came in many shapes and sizes. It was important to store food for traveling and the hard times that could come. Some pots were plain, but others were carved and painted with images or geometric designs in beautiful colors.

YOU WILL NEED

- self-hardening clay (available at craft supply stores)
- a plate
- acrylic paint and a paintbrush

1 Take as much clay as will fit between your cupped hands. Roll it into a ball. Set the ball down firmly on the plate so that the clay flattens a bit at the bottom.

2 Poke or pinch your thumbs into the center of the clay ball. Squeeze your thumbs on the inside together with your fingers on the outside of the walls of the pot.

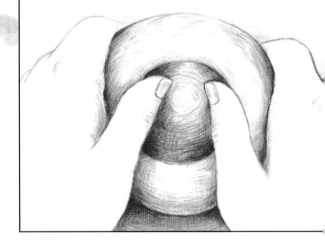

3 Continue to shape the pot, pinching and turning the clay with your thumbs and fingers. If the clay feels dry, moisten your fingers with water.

4 When the walls of the pot are bowl-shaped and even, wet your fingers and smooth the surfaces of the pot as well as the rim. Let the pot dry in a warm place for a day.

5 When the pot looks and feels dry, gently twist it away from the plate. Turn the pot upside down and let the bottom dry.

6 Paint the bottom of the pot first. Paint past the bottom, onto the sides a little. Leave the pot upside down on the plate to dry.

7 Paint the inside of the pot and set it on the plate to dry. When the inside is dry, paint the outside and let it dry. You may need at least two coats of paint.

OTHER IDEAS

• Carefully use the edge of a knife to press lines and designs into the pot when the clay is wet.

• Paint animals such as deer or birds on the outside or the inside of the pot.

Painted pouch

Pouches might have held fire-making tools or whetstones for sharpening knives. The Hidatsa wore a small pouch tied around the waist. The Cheyenne used buffalo-hide pouches called parfleches to store meat. Other large parfleches held clothing or blankets. Many pouches would be brightly decorated with paint, quills or beading.

YOU WILL NEED

- a pencil and ruler
- a large piece of felt
- scissors • a needle and thread
- yarn
- acrylic paint and a paintbrush

1 Draw a 20 cm x 14 cm (8 in. x 6 in.) rectangle on the felt and cut it out. Cut out a second rectangle measuring 17 cm x 14 cm (7 in. x 6 in.).

2 Lay the small rectangle on the large one, leaving 5 cm (2 in.) at the bottom as shown.

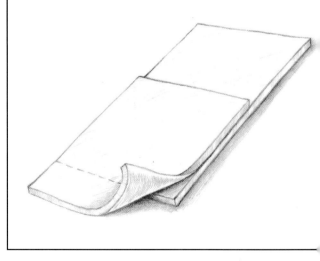

3 Thread the needle and knot the end of the doubled thread. Using overlapping or blanket stitches, sew the two pieces of felt together down both sides.

6 Cut three lengths of yarn, each at least 50 cm (20 in.) long. Tie them together at one end, braid them and knot the other end.

4 The bottom of the pouch is the end with the smaller flap. Sew the two pieces of felt together at the flap.

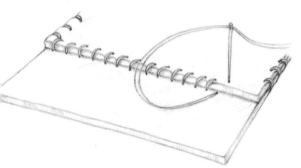

7 Sew each end of the braided strap to the pouch just inside the corners of the closing flap.

5 Cut the entire bottom flap into fringes. Cut 2.5-cm (1-in.) fringes into the larger flap. Fold the large flap over to close the pouch.

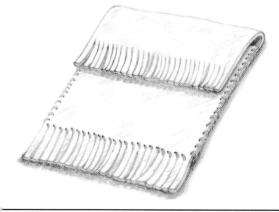

8 Paint the pouch with designs, animals or flowers.

Totem pole

Some Aboriginal peoples used totem poles to tell about their family histories or to honor important members. Totem poles placed at the front of a house displayed family crests. Other totems, called welcome figures, stood on beaches to greet visitors. Tlingit, Kwakiutl and Tsimshian families hired talented carvers who studied long years to perfect their craft.

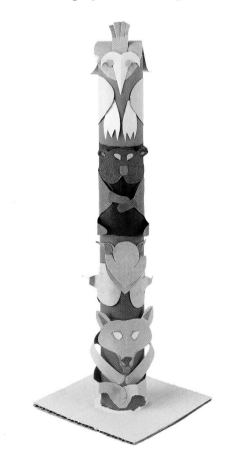

1 Draw three evenly spaced lines around the circumference of the tube or dowel. Paint each section a different color and let the paint dry. Your totem figures will fit into these sections.

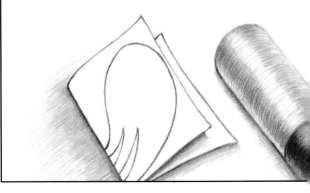

2 Decide on the figures for the totem. You can use people or animals that are important to you.

3 Cut a piece of construction paper the same height as one of the totem sections and fold it in half. Along the edge of the fold, draw half the body shape of one of your totem figures.

4 With the paper still folded, cut out the figure. Glue the body onto the pole, making the tail, wings or paws stick out.

5 Cut out a face for your figure and glue it on. Add paper eyes, a nose and other details.

6 Repeat steps 3 to 5 for each of the other three totem figures.

7 Cut out an 8 cm x 8 cm (3 in. x 3 in.) cardboard square for the base of the totem pole and paint it.

8 When the base is dry, spread glue around the bottom of the totem. Glue the pole onto the base. Hold the pole or prop it against something so that it dries straight.

Moccasins

Footwear varied depending on the climate and the materials available. For northern winters, the Aleut had mukluks or boots. Far to the south, the Pima made rawhide sandals. The Chippewa and Kutchin wore hide moccasins that could be attached to leggings. Footwear was beaded, painted or fringed.

YOU WILL NEED

- newspaper
- a marker and ruler   • scissors
- felt or other soft, durable fabric
- acrylic or fabric paint and a paintbrush
- a needle and thread
- pins   • ribbon

1 Draw an outline of your foot on the newspaper and cut out this pattern.

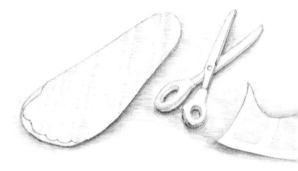

2 Place your pattern on the felt or fabric and draw around it for the sole of the moccasin. Leave at least 2.5 cm (1 in.) all around the pattern. Cut out the sole.

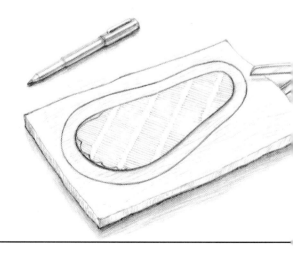

3 At the heel, mark and cut two slits as wide apart as your heel is wide and 2.5 cm (1 in.) long.

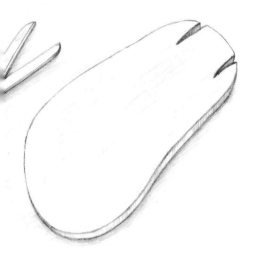

4 Place your pattern on the felt and draw the upper piece for the moccasin. It should be a bit wider over your instep and about half the length of your foot. Cut it out.

5 Follow steps 2 to 4 to cut out pieces for the second moccasin.

6 For each cuff, cut out a piece of felt that is 2.5 cm (1 in.) wide and as long as the sole of the moccasin.

7 Paint designs on the cuffs and uppers. Let them dry.

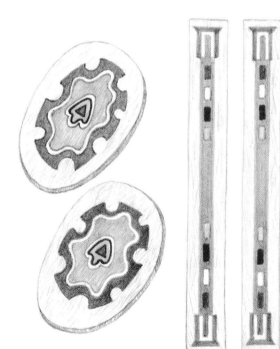

Instructions continue on the next page ☞

8 Sew a running or gathering stitch around the front part of the sole, starting at the instep.

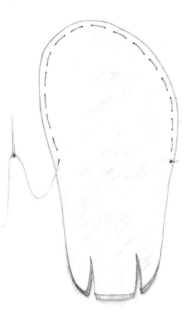

10 Fold the side flaps one over the other and sew them together to make the heel seam. Cut the heel flap into a rounded shape and sew it to the heel.

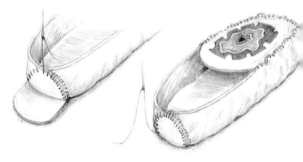

11 Sew on the cuff.

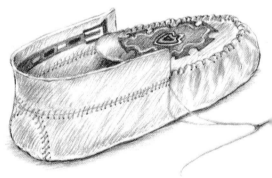

9 Pin the upper section to the sole as shown. Pull the gathering thread until the sole fits the shape of the upper. Sew the upper onto the sole.

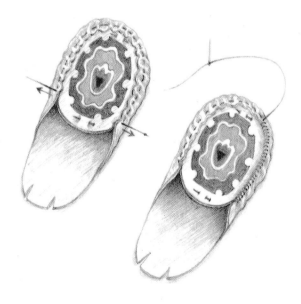

12 Cut four slits on each side of the moccasin, as shown.

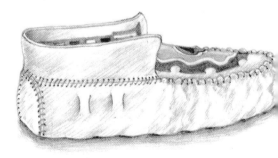

13 For a drawstring, cut a piece of ribbon that reaches around the cuff. The ribbon should be long enough to tie in a bow or loose knot.

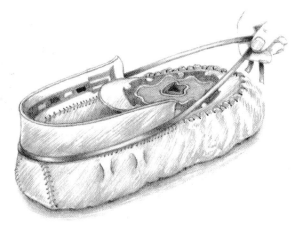

14 Sew the ribbon to the back of the heel under the cuff and thread it through the slits on each side of the moccasin. Fold down the cuff.

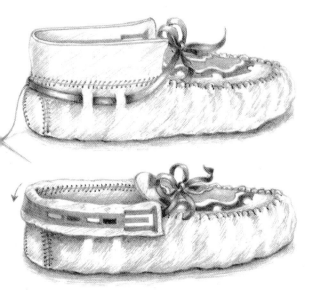

15 Repeat steps 8 to 14 to make the second moccasin.

OTHER IDEAS

• Use thread or yarn, instead of paint, to embroider a design on the front of the moccasin.

• Sew feathers or strings of beads to the back of cuffs.

• Make the cuffs wider and cut them into fringes.

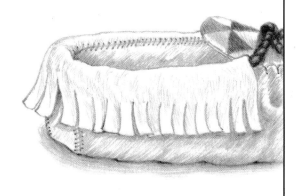

Cornhusk doll

Aboriginal peoples have grown corn, or maize, for thousands of years. After the harvest, parts of the corn could be used for things besides food. The Nez Perce wove fine bags and cornhusk mats. The Seneca even made moccasins with husks. Many people still make cornhusk and corncob dolls. Here is how to make a cornhusk doll like the ones the Penobscot crafted. A traditional cornhusk doll has no face.

YOU WILL NEED

- two large ears of corn
- a knife • scissors and a ruler
- yarn • white glue
- fabric scraps and thin ribbon
- a needle and thread
- acrylic paint and a small paintbrush

1 With the help of an adult, cut the stalks from the cobs and remove the husks. Spread out the husks and let them dry for two or three days. (Save one of the cobs to make the corncob doll on page 29.)

2 Soak the dry husks in warm water for 10 or 15 minutes to soften them.

3 Bundle six leaves together and tie the pointed ends together with a long, thin strip of cornhusk. Double knot the strip.

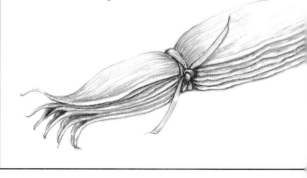

4 Carefully peel the leaves back to form the head. Tightly tie a thin strip of cornhusk where you want the neck to be. Double knot the strip.

5 For the arms, split a long cornhusk into three lengths. Tie the lengths together at one end with a strip of husk. Braid the lengths and tie the other end of the braid with a strip of husk.

6 Braid two more pieces as in step 5 and tie them together to make legs.

7 Fit the arm piece in under the neck. Roll a small ball of cornhusk and stuff it inside the body under the arms. Tie a strip of cornhusk at the doll's waist.

8 Insert the legs under the waist. Tie them in place with some of the strips that are hanging down from the body.

Instructions continue on the next page ☞

9 For hair, cut thirty lengths of yarn each about 18 cm (7 in.) long. Loosely tie the yarn in the middle of the lengths. This makes the center part in the hair.

10 Tie off the hair on each side about 2.5 cm (1 in.) from the center part. Braid each hair section and tie the ends with yarn or ribbon. Glue the hair onto the doll's head.

11 For a skirt, cut a strip of fabric about 18 cm (7 in.) wide and long enough to reach from the doll's waist to its ankles. Sew a running stitch along the top of the skirt.

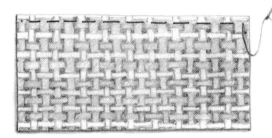

12 Wrap the fabric around the doll. Gather the fabric by pulling the thread tightly and tie the skirt around the doll's waist.

13 To make a shawl, cut a strip of fabric about 2.5 cm x 15 cm (1 in. x 6 in.). Wrap it across the doll's shoulders and around its waist. Tie the shawl in place at the waist with ribbon.

Corncob doll

3 For hair, loosely wind yarn around your hand in 30 loops. Cut the loops at each end and tie them off at one end to make bangs. Glue the hair onto the doll's head.

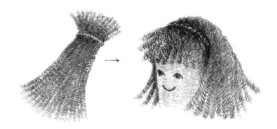

4 Trim the yarn so that the hair is shoulder length and even. Tie a headband of ribbon around the doll's head.

1 For supplies see the list of materials and step 1 on page 26. Have an adult help you cut the corn and the stalk off the cob. Let the cob dry for a few days.

5 Follow steps 11 and 12 on page 28 to make the skirt.

6 The blouse is made the same way as the skirt. Cut the fabric wide enough so that it will hang over the top of the skirt. Tie ribbon around the top of the blouse.

2 Paint on a face.

Clay doll

Some dolls were used in ceremonies and treasured from generation to generation, but many dolls were children's well-loved toys. Apache and Dakota children had dolls sewn from animal hide. The Yuma and Mohave people made dolls from clay. No matter what materials were used to make dolls, they were often carefully painted and dressed to look like their owners.

YOU WILL NEED

- self hardening clay
(available at craft supply stores)
- toothpicks   • 5 paper clips
- acrylic paint and a paintbrush
- yarn   • scissors, a ruler and white glue
- fabric scraps and thin ribbon
- a needle and thread   • seed beads

1 For the body, mold a lump of clay that fits into the palm of your hand into an oblong shape. Roll out four sausage shapes for arms and legs. The legs should be longer and thicker than the arms.

2 Roll a clay ball for the head. Squeeze the clay on each side of the head to make the ears. With a wet toothpick, pierce each earlobe, twisting the toothpick as you pass it in and out. Make sure the holes are large enough for beads to pass through.

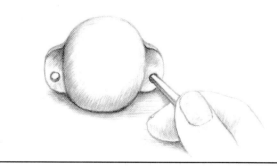

3 Add a small piece of clay to the head for the nose. Wet your fingers and smooth it onto the face.

4 Unbend the paper clips. Push them into the body where you will attach the head, arms and legs. Press the head, arms and legs onto the paper clips until they touch the body. Smooth the clay so that no joints show. Let the doll dry for a few days.

5 Paint on designs to decorate the doll's face, arms and legs. For the hair, see steps 3 and 4 on page 29.

6 For the skirt, cut a piece of fabric 18 cm (7 in.) wide and long enough to reach from under the doll's arms to its ankles. Sew a running stitch along the top of the fabric. Use the thread to tie the skirt around the doll.

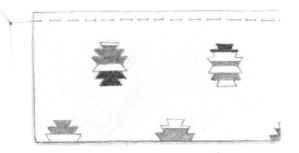

7 For earrings, thread the needle and string on beads. When there are enough beads to make a small circle, cut the thread, run it through the ear hole and tie it.

8 Thread a string of beads for a necklace and double loop it around the doll's neck. Tie the ends together.

Bullroarer

The Pueblo made groaning sticks or bullroarers. The Inupiat had a similar device called a wolf scare. A bullroarer was carved from the wood of a tree that had been struck by lightning. The wolf scare was made from the baleen of whales and a piece of walrus tusk. When you spin either object around your head, it makes a sound like the moaning of the wind or the howling of a wolf.

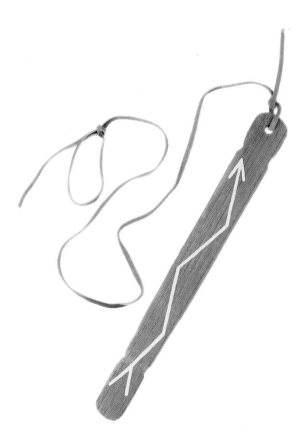

YOU WILL NEED

- a paint stirrer from a hardware or paint store, or a piece of wood about 30 cm (12 in.) long, 4 cm (1½ in.) wide and 0.5 cm (¼ in.) thick
- sandpaper • a drill
- acrylic paint and a paintbrush
- 60 cm (24 in.) of heavy cord or leather lace

1 Sand the wood smooth on all sides.

2 Have an adult drill a hole near one end of the wood that is large enough for the cord to pass through. If you are using a paint stirrer, there may already be a hole in one end.

3 Paint designs on each side of the wood. Thunderbird or lightning symbols could be used, but you can make up your own designs with stripes or geometric shapes as well.

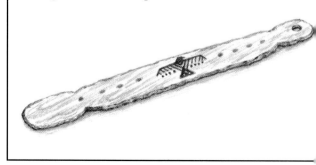

4 When the paint is dry, run the cord or lace through the hole. Tie it tightly with a double knot. Tie a hand loop, if you like.

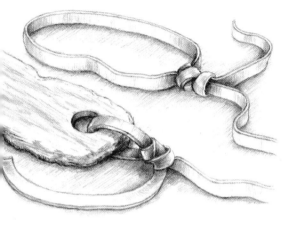

5 To make the bullroarer roar, take it outside to an open area away from other people and swing it in circles around your head or at your side.

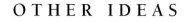

OTHER IDEAS

• To decorate the bullroarer so that it looks like a wolf scare, paint wolves and other Arctic animals on each side.

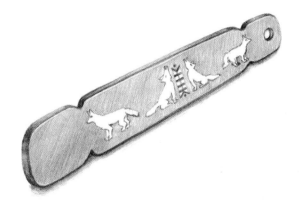

• Make a handle for the bullroarer by having an adult drill a hole through the center of a short piece of dowel. Thread the bullroarer's cord or lace through the hole and tightly double knot it.

Rasp

All sorts of musical instruments were used to accompany the singing and dancing that took place during ceremonies or celebrations. The Haida made finely carved whistles. The Hopi and Zuni played flutes of cane, reed and wood. Many peoples carved rasps from lengths of wood.

1   Sand both pieces of wood until they are smooth.

2   Have an adult help you carefully cut evenly spaced notches along both edges of the paint stirrer for the rasp.

3 Paint a pattern of designs, shapes or colors on the areas of the rasp that are not notched. Let them dry.

4 Paint designs on the playing stick at the end you will hold while playing. Let them dry.

5 To play the rasp, run the playing stick across the notched edges.

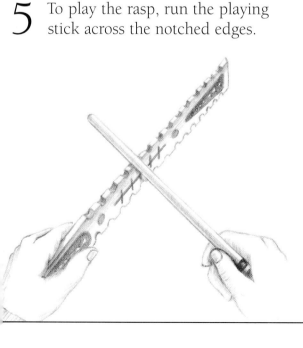

OTHER IDEAS

• Tie feathers or strings of beads onto one end of the rasp.

• To make a different sound, hold the rasp close to the opening of an overturned drum as you play it.

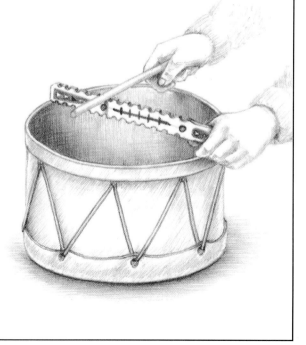

Turtle rattle

Drums, rattles and voices were used to make music for many occasions. The Tlingit carved ornate rattles from wood in the shapes of animals, birds and people. The Makah strung scallop shells together on leather thongs to make rattles. Hollowed-out gourds filled with pebbles were made by many peoples. With the shells of box turtles and snapping turtles, the Seneca made several kinds of beautiful rattles.

1 Sand the stick or dowel until it is smooth. Paint it, making one end look like the head of a turtle. Let it dry.

2 Put the plates together facing each other. Holding them in place, trim the paper so the round plates become more oval and scalloped.

3 Paint one plate to be the turtle's back. With different colors, paint the other plate to look like the turtle's belly. Let the plates dry.

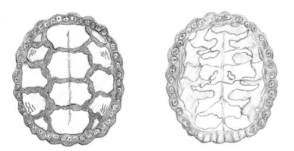

4 Hold the plates together. Cut two small slits on either side where the neck and tail of the handle will stick out. This will allow the edges of the plates to fit over the stick.

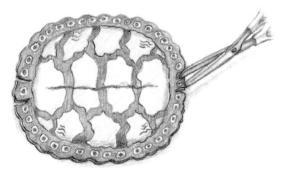

5 Spread glue on the inside edge of the bottom plate. Put in a few pebbles or beans.

6 Lay the stick on the bottom plate with the head poking out. Keep the slits on either side of the stick. Set the top plate over the stick.

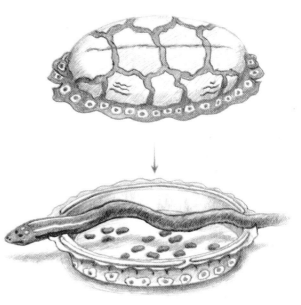

7 Hold the plates together with clothespins until the glue has dried.

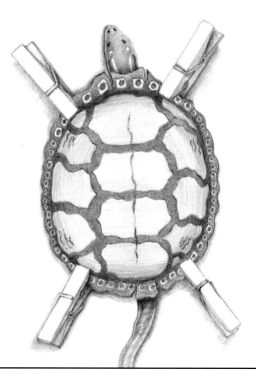

Hoop drum

Many Aboriginal people say that the sound of a drum is the sound of a beating heart. Some drums were used for ceremonies and other drums were beaten during dancing. The Cherokee and Oneida made water drums of wood and animal skin. An Inuit drum would belong to the entire village. Today, the singing and drumming at gatherings or powwows create an unforgettable sound.

1 Have an adult remove the bottom of the cookie tin with the can opener.

2 Cut a piece of shelf paper the same circumference and width as the tin. Peel off the backing and stick the paper on the tin.

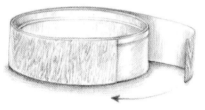

3 Spread the leather out, smooth side down. Set the tin on the leather and trace a circle about 2.5 cm (1 in.) bigger than the tin. Cut out the circle.

4 Mark 12 evenly spaced dots around the edge of the rough side of the leather, about 2.5 cm (1 in.) in from the edge. Use the knife to carefully poke holes in the leather at these dots.

5 Cut the leather lace into six equal pieces. Soak the laces and the leather circle in warm water for about 15 minutes, until they soften.

6 Take the laces and leather out of the water and pat them dry. Thread a lace through one of the holes in the leather. Double knot the lace, leaving a length hanging.

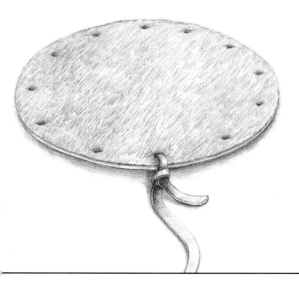

7 Place the cookie tin on the center of the leather on the rough side. Stretch the lace across the bottom of the drum and thread it up through the hole that is across from where the lace is tied. Pull it tight and double knot it. Thread and tie the next three laces the same way, pulling the leather tight but being careful not to tear it.

8 As you pull the last two laces across the bottom of the drum, wrap them around the other laces where they cross in the center. Tie the laces tightly.

9 Set the drum in a warm place to dry for a few days. As the leather dries, it will shrink and tighten. Turn the page to make the drumstick, or drum beater.

Drum beater

YOU WILL NEED

- a 23-cm (9-in.) square of leather
- some pebbles
- a stick or dowel about
  30 cm (12 in.) long
- a 20-cm (8-in.) length of leather lace

1 Cut out a circle of leather with a diameter of about 10 cm (4 in.).

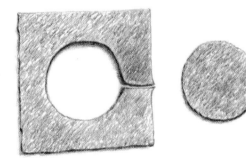

2 Put a few pebbles into the center of the rough side of the leather.

3 Set the stick onto the center of the leather and gather the leather around it.

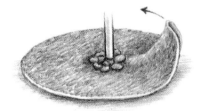

4 Wrap the lace tightly around the stick and the leather several times. Double knot the lace in place.

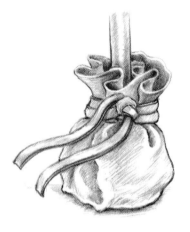

OTHER IDEAS

- Tie feathers to the laces on the drum or to the handle of the drum beater.

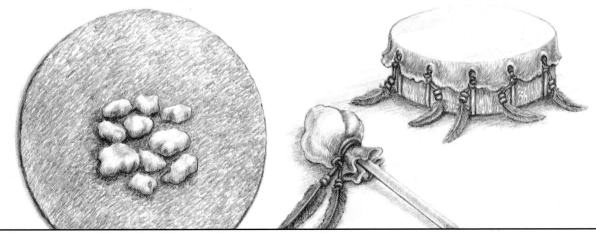